Curly to the Rescue

Tony Mitton

Illustrated by Jo Brooker

Photographed by Keith Lil

RIGBY

"Come up, little ladybird,"
said the spider.
"Come up and see me."

"Come up, green grasshopper,"
said the spider.
"Come up and see me."

"Come up, big beetle,"
said the spider.
"Come up and see me."

The spider smiled.
"Hee hee!" she said.
"Now I will eat the ladybird
and the grasshopper and
the beetle for my tea."

Along came Curly.
"**Help!**" said the ladybird.
"**Help!**" said the grasshopper.
"**Help! Help!**" said the beetle.
"**The spider is going to eat us!**"

Curly saw the snail.
"Help!" he said.
"The spider is going to eat the ladybird and the grasshopper and the beetle!"

Curly and the snail
pulled on the web.
Down came the web!

"Hurray!" said the ladybird and the grasshopper and the beetle. They all ran away.